FORGIVE YOURSELF

YOURSELF

THESE TINY ACTS OF
SELF-DESTRUCTION

T0025555

FORGIVE YOURSELF

THESE TINY ACTS OF SELF-DESTRUCTION

poems by

Jared Singer

© 2019 by Jared Singer

Published by Button Poetry / Exploding Pinecone Press

Minneapolis, MN 55403 | http://www.buttonpoetry.com

All Rights Reserved

Manufactured in the United States of America

Cover design: David Benthal

ISBN 978-1-943735-61-7

Angels aren't a mythic creation. They aren't perfect beings created by an unknowable power. Angels are people who are able to set aside their fear, pain, and baggage to be just a little more of the kinder part of human for someone else. Even if only for a little while.

This book is dedicated to the three angels without whom I would never have made it. Tiffany Woodley. Ben Baynton. Rico Frederick. You are the examples I live by. Thank you for loving me for all of my small faults and forgiving my big ones.

CONTENTS

FORGIVE YOURSELF

THESE TINY ACTS OF SELF-DESTRUCTION

HOMETOWN

I only go back to where I was raised to celebrate
or mourn. It is getting hard to tell the difference between
funerals and weddings. Laughing and crying look the
same from a distance. There are long meaningful
embraces at both. I wear the same suit,

only the tie changes. We raise the first glass of the night
to a memory no matter what. The only difference?
Whether or not there will be fewer of us next time.

SHATTER

This is for everyone who ever thought
Gd gave me this blood, so surely if I choose to spill it,
learn to bathe in it, that must make me holy, right?
Nothing else has worked.

This is for everyone who fell in love with the let go—
who cut and cut and cut
but never gave in to the give up—
who never killed themselves.

This is for those who, at the bottom of the well,
chose to live. Thank you—
you taught me honesty in a way that teachers
and parents never considered.

I never made a mark on my own body—
instead I stood proud and
let someone else do the breaking.
Called it football,
called it dirt bike,
called it round here you take
a beating when you earn it, boy,
called it do your worst, I know you can't
break me half as hard I deserve to be broken.

Every injury just another opportunity to learn
to love this body. After all, calcium deposits
are always stronger the second time around.
This body is no mere temple of stone to be easily
shattered. I made it life-strong one break at a time.

Baptism is the process of making the mundane holy.
When you learn that you can do that yourself,
there is no more need for the stand-proud.

You can put down the blade made
perfect by your blood. Set aside the fury
until you really need it.

I am unbreakable.

I
  have
    learned
   to
  bend.

JARED (   ) SINGER

The act of naming something
is an attempt to give it purpose.

When someone wants you to be
anything but what you are,
the easiest way to start
is with a nickname.

(Motek): the Hebrew word for the masculine
version of sweetheart. She wanted me to be
more Jewish and more hers.

(Patsy): half legend, half job description.
I took all the blame. For the cigarettes, the booze,
the broken window, the fist.
I was the good kid, the one parents wouldn't hate.
I was willing to take all the blame,
just to be a part of someone else's story.

(Son): not given by father.
Every adult man who wants you
to be more like them will call you son,
usually when giving instructions.
If they think their daughter may be
serious about you, this name becomes
half promise and half threat.

(Marley): as in Jacob Marley,
the first ghost to visit Scrooge.
As in Jew Boy, the only way
you will be a part of our story is as
a cautionary tale, forever
wrapped in chains and money
boxes. At first, this was just a name
I assumed for a school play.

4

But when they see how well
you carry a burden, a stereotype,
it will remain forever yours.

(J): a shortening of my first name,
inconsequential and meaningless,
I hated this nickname. Trading
in my whole person for a letter.
When I complained they laughed.

I wouldn't let them see me break.
So I pretended this wasn't a surrender
of me. Called it a new chance, a chance
to make something beautiful with
this building block of a word. Maybe
I could be a bird. Fragile, magnificent.

WHY I WILL NEVER LEARN TO PLAY THE CELLO

Some things are holy enough
that they deserve to only be done
well. Love, cello, forgiveness.

I am too much engineer, too
gearheart to hold something without
trying to improve it.

The broad hips of the cello
don't need improving.
Its maple does not need improving.

The slow drag of bow
across string reminds
me too much of breathing
to do both at the same time.

There is not enough bend in
my whole body to twist a note
like that.

I envy those willing to ineptly
tackle the holy. Fledgling priests,
high school sweethearts, new cellists.
I did not need anyone to tell me
that music and faith are synonyms.

Dirtfinger calloushand gearheart that I am
I knew from the first time I heard the cello
chase all the other strings into echo
that I would never play one.
Instead I build concert halls.
Instead I engineer the music.
I cannot bend, but it is the music
that lets me stand straight.

EXCHANGE RATES

Certain Norse tribes believed
that all human beings were created exactly equal—
that from the moment we first draw breath, we
are unconsciously trading one attribute for another.
That there is an absolute limit to human potential.

Nothing can be gained without equal sacrifice.
That, by definition, a great beauty can
never be a mighty warrior.

These same people believed that singers
tap into the same power that the gods do,
that to be able to uplift only with your voice
is the closest thing to magic left in this world.

I used to be able sing,
but I traded in my last gasp of magic
for the gravel in my throat,
for the steel in my belly.
I am not a great beauty.
I will never be a mighty warrior
or a masterful sage.

I traded in all my potential for tenacity.
I don't want to be mediocre forever—
how much did I sacrifice for all these second chances?
I don't want to have to try so hard for so little
forever.
I need to know—

is it possible to trade back in,
to give up this steel
for something softer,
something easier to hold?

AN AUTOBIOGRAPHY

The boy who wears his comic books like armor often sits
alone. He is more comfortable with Iron Man and his
own thoughts than he will ever be with a woman.
Because of his nervous ticks, no matter how long they
are together, she will never feel commonplace to him.
She will always know she is special.

The boy who wears his comic books like armor
tries to tell her that he loves her every day.
She does not understand.
When he says, *You remind me of Psylocke,*
he is not saying he actually thinks
she is a scantily clad assassin.
He is just saying, *Damn girl, you must be psychic.*
How else could you always know the right thing
to make me smile? You have to be a ninja.
How else could you have stolen my heart so easily?
He is saying, *Dammmmmmmmmnnnnnnn girl,*
you absolutely have to be Psylocke!
She is the only character I have ever read about
who is as graceful and daring as you are.
She does not understand.

The boy who wears his comic books like armor
is not a good lover. The way he barely touches
her makes her feel unattractive.
Like he is only doing this because she wants him to.
This could not be further from the truth.
He is simply treating her like the only thing
that has ever been this important to him before:
comic books.

He removes her clothes like he would
the slipcover from a brand new issue,

as careful not to wrinkle her clothing
as he is not to damage the plastic.

One day, she will leave him because feeling special isn't
as important as feeling loved. He does love her.
She can't understand. He will spend the rest of his life
wishing he were Peter Parker, knowing that if he had a
mask to remove, then, just like Mary Jane, she would be
with him forever. But he doesn't have a mask to remove,

just an awkward smile.
He hopes that one day
that's enough.

SIMPLE TRUTH

I run into the first woman who ever saw me naked
at a wedding with her husband.
He looks nothing like I do. But she holds
him just like she held me.

Her hands on his body
where my scars are—
love is eternal.

And sometimes unspeakably brutal.

MY HANDS

are dirty
and calloused.
No, not dirty—

I can feel the rust that
has leeched into them
slowly replacing my marrow.

Every scar a
reminder of my
ability to hold on

long after the let-go
became the logical choice.
I don't mind

becoming all the things
my hands have held.
This is the point

of callouses. To be
tool-sharp, hard,
and still human.

THERE IS A WOLF IN MY CHEST

I think there is supposed to be an organ
where he lives. It's hard to remember over
all that growling.

Lone wolves almost always
follow their former pack,
protecting them. They
never live more
than a year.

There is no pack in my body,
too many bones, too much blood,
not enough moons to howl at.

But the wolf in my chest is alive and well.
He eats when I starve,
heartbreak his regular meal.
Love, his long winter.

Even exiled, the lone wolf howls
when his pack is threatened.
Whenever a woman
feels possible, he roars
and scratches until I give up.

His year is almost over,
the mourning period
finished. I wonder what will
take his place.

A scavenger? Or rot?
Will a new heart grow from
his cave?

It is spring now,
when wolves and men alike
get another chance.

THE LAST TIME WE SAW EACH OTHER

No matter how many friends you bury
it never gets easier, but it does become automatic.

The last time we saw each other,
we were both four hours deep into
celebrating a redneck wedding,
which is to say, so full of whiskey,
barbeque, and Jell-O shots
that good decisions were an impossibility.
On any other day we would have walked
right by each other.

But no matter how much we think we have
taught our eyes about lying, whiskey
has much more to teach our
tongues about the truth.

With barely any preamble, you asked me
why I turned you down in the sixth grade.
I said *pretty girls used to scare me,*
they kinda still do.

I asked you why you turned me down in the tenth grade.
You said *pride—what kind of woman*
would you be if you went back to the first
boy who broke your heart?

You asked if you should call.
I asked if I should visit.
We both fell back into our whiskey,

neither of us thinking
this would be the last time
we didn't say goodbye.

SIDESHOW

I am learning to breathe fire.
When asked why, I say, *I want to
be half dragon. Who doesn't?*

This is true, but only part of the story.
If I am half legend, then I am only half human.
Only half fallible. *Who doesn't want that also?*

EXCHANGE RATES 2

Certain Norse tribes believed
that all human beings were created exactly equal,
that from the moment we first draw breath, we
are unconsciously trading in one attribute for another.
That there is an absolute limit to human potential.
Nothing can be gained without equal sacrifice.

I think I traded in all my potential for tenacity—
how much did I sacrifice for all my second chances?
I think I traded in all my magic for the gravel in my
throat, for the steel in my belly.

I used to be ashamed of this.
I wanted to know if I could trade all of this in
for something softer.

I had not yet learned the magic of steel,
did not yet know how everything echoes in here,
had not learned the different sound my bones make
after failure and success.

I thought being hard to hold was always a fault.
When I finally melt, I fit perfectly.
I will not fall when leaned on.

I make this melt beautiful.
I make this grate, grind,
and spark respectable.

The Norse were wrong
about at least one thing—
there is magic in this too.

TO THE BOY WITH THE BROKEN SKIN
for Lewis Kleiner

For most of us,
our skin only records
our traumatic moments and our obsessions.

My body only remembers
broken bones, too-tall fences,
and my religion.
I will never let it forget.
Her body remembers only a C-section and
that one time she grabbed a hot pot barehanded.

But your broken skin
remembers your every movement
better than the most detailed journal.

Like that time your cat scratched you—
didn't even break the skin.
You even have scars from sunburns.
Never thought that would be something I'd
be jealous of.

It is our memories that make us
who we are. The rest of us have to cling
to them like life vests or hope.

Your body does the work for you.
You are the only person I have ever met
who gets to *just* be.

HARDEST THING

I think we should redefine tragedy
as that which is impossible to get over.
Unless you are *profoundly* lucky,
it will happen to you.

Holding the body of someone you love
who has committed suicide
is easy. All you have to do is sit
while you wait for the paramedics and hope
that you are wrong, pray
that there is still a person to save.

When you are in shock, the weight
of a torso is negligible. For all the strain
it puts on your body, you may as well
be on the beach holding a book.

On that day when all your happy daydreams
seem tiny and all your nightmares huge.
On the day when the worst *what if* that you can imagine
has already happened—when a friend commits suicide,
when your stepfather is paralyzed,
maybe forever—whatever your tragedy is,

please use me as a cautionary tale.
Only a madman tries to do the impossible.
After her death, I was indeed a madman.

I tried to get over her death. Failing that,
I did nothing.

I sat in my own filth for three weeks
until a dear friend walked into my room
carrying a towel, hoping I was not another
impossible task. He said, *You are taking a shower*

right now.
That shower is the hardest thing I have ever done.

You can't get over someone,
but you can take a shower
and then you can get dressed
and then you can do your laundry
and then you can find your keys
and then you can go grocery shopping
and then it's ten years later
and they are still dead

and you are happy.

I don't believe in Gd, but I do believe in miracles,
in things so large that they seem impossible
but when you do them one tiny step at a time
you get them done.
Taking a shower is a miracle.
Laughing is a miracle.
Being *here* is a miracle.

We all give up. We all hide.
We all wallow in our own whatever awful
we have to wallow in. But if you're lucky,
you can find a miracle. Take a shower.
Keep doing tiny things until the world is
a slightly less dark place.

FOR CHRISTINE (MY BEST FRIEND'S FIANCÉE)

I haven't known you very long,
but you look at him the same way I do,
the same way his mother does.

You are less lover than hawk.
I can tell from your shoulder hunch,
the way your hands are never occupied,
that you are always ready to plummet,
to kill in the manner Gd intended.

I am only sure of your purpose,
never your intent. I don't know
if you are planning to disembowel
my friend the moment he steps out of line
or consume anyone who might threaten him.

I am sure, however, that as meticulous
as you are, you would clean yourself perfectly,
clean your hands and change before anyone
would notice.

I like you this way.
He needs someone to watch over him.
It can't be me or his mother.
We both love him too gentle to even
consider that he might be the threat to himself.

RESONANCE

My mother's birthday
is the same day someone
I know was murdered.

I call her every year
to wish her a happy birthday,
but I can never manage to sound happy.

Buying her flowers
always feels like buying a
funeral bouquet and sending
it to the wrong house.

FIRST KISS MAGIC

I have always found it easier to believe
in broken teeth than love.

There is a girl who thinks
it's inappropriate to kiss
me under a street lamp.
She does it anyway,
my mouth is full of crowns.

I feel like Peter Pan some days.
I know it's impossible,
but I believe even this body can fly—
like every broken bone,
every bruise, is a feather.

If they had told the story right,
Captain Hook would not have been an old man,
simply a mirror.
Nothing can take away our will to
fly faster than we can.

Tell me I am not 300 plus pounds of wingspan, mirror.
Tell me I am not dirty whiskey angel, mirror.
Tell me I am still earthbound, mirror.

You dirty liar.

THE ENGINEER SEEKS ARTISTRY

The engineer researches metaphor,
understands its definition, but not its chemical
composition. This presents problems;
he considers solving them by cataloging all of literature.

Citing practicality concerns, he decides
to create not a metaphor,
but metaphor itself, out of
basic building blocks. He starts by making it
all flat surfaces and right angles, assuming
that it is easier to compare something
if it is close to you. He makes
it out of metal, burnishes it to a mirror finish,
believing that if its surface reflects what
is in front of it, then half the work of
the metaphor is already done.

The engineer tries to use his new creation
to make a simple metaphor. Fails.
Frustrated, he throws it to the ground and stomps
until, like all things, it bends under human anger.
The more he crushes it, the more he realizes it looks
like a house. No, his house. The one he grew up in.
The metaphors flood unasked for, like all the science
is gone from his brain and this is all that's left. He has no
idea how copper can look so much like brick.
No idea how metal can smell so much like skinned knees
and family dinners.
Confused, but knowing he succeeded,
the engineer sets aside metaphor, rightly afraid
to handle it too much.

ON BEING A FAT MAN

All the regular men on the subway
take up as much space as they can.
When standing, hands are on hips,
elbows extended, like they are a flag
planted penis-first in the ground, and
therefore it is theirs. When sitting,
they take up even more space, legs
spread all the way as if to say, *See how
easily I conquer.*

As a fat man, I take up as much space as
they do without even trying, so I try to make
myself as small as possible, hands folded over my
enormous belly, elbows at my side,
my knees bolted together. I don't know if this
makes me less of a man or more self-conscious.
I would like to believe it means I am more
polite, but I doubt it.

When you are a successful fat man,
that is what you will always be.
You will never just be successful or
just a man.

I HAVE NEVER BEEN SUICIDAL,

never wanted to kill myself.

I have always believed that life is a gift.
Sometimes it's a gift you don't want,

an itchy sweater you wish you could return.
I have never wanted to kill myself,

but I have wanted to die.
Prayed for it.

I have always felt that suicide
was the ultimate disrespect

to all who wanted to live and were taken anyway—
spit in the face of those left behind.

I'd always thought that despair
would feel empty. That's how it's

always described. It isn't—
it is full and terror-cold.

I am happier than I have ever been.
I still have a hard time believing in myself,
use the word *broken* too much.
I have never been suicidal, but now I love the living.
I stopped looking at life as good or bad, a series
of snapshots where each was either a reason
to live or a reason to die.
I have not always wanted to live. For a long time I
couldn't even imagine what joy would feel like.
It's a melody. It's a tide. It is full and warm.

A LETTER TO SARAH
CONTEMPLATING SUPERPOWERS

If I could regenerate any damage to my body,
I would double backflip belly flop
off the tallest building I could find.
I would make you watch.
Would not tell you it won't kill me.
When my body hits the ground,
turns bone to dust,
when blood splatters across your face,
there will be a moment
when your heart stops,
when the belly drops out of your everything.
I would calmly walk over to you and say,
Yeah, ever since you killed yourself,
it's been like that for all of us.
All of the time.

If I could fly,
I would take you so high so fast
you would be terrified that wind resistance
alone would rip you out of my arms.
Don't worry. I would hold on to you
with a strength born of fear and longing.
When your vision starts to go black, I will whisper,
If you'd only told us something was wrong
we could've held you,
told you we loved you.
We could have helped.

If I could read people's minds,
I would not invade your privacy.
Instead, I would eavesdrop on every passerby,
tattoo my arms with all the compliments,
every *wow she's good looking,*

every *I wish I was that confident.*
Meeting all of your ex-lovers
would turn my chest and back into a masterpiece.
Recording every *how could I have ever let her get away?*
every *she was the best thing that ever happened to me.*
My legs would turn into a patchwork of hatch marks
for every time I wished you were still with me.
It wouldn't even take a day to cover this body
with all of the nice things people didn't think
you needed to hear.

If I could travel through time, I would go back
to the moment before it was too late.
Right before you wrote a suicide note that started
Dear Jared:
I'm doing this now because I know you will be the one to
find me. Of all of my friends, I think you're the one who's
strong enough to take it.
What made you think I was strong enough to take this?
I would go back to the moment before you
became the reason I don't read letters
without having someone else proofread them first.

If I could project my thoughts into another's head,
even knowing it could never have saved you
but believing maybe it could have saved me,
you would never have doubted,
even for an instant,
that you were loved.

BEING JEWISH MEANS ALWAYS BEING TOO MUCH OR NOT ENOUGH 1

It's the 4th of July, a day meant to celebrate
freedom and tolerance in a country that seems
to have forgotten both.

There is less to celebrate every year, but
we have the day off and most of us still
have hope that the country can be made better.
So we throw a party, not for our country's birth,
but for each other.

I invite all my friends in the city, even those
I know can't come. I want to let the people
I care about know it, every time I can.

Among those who come is the Good Man.
He is the first to laugh, the first to pour someone
else a drink, and always, always, the first to give
you a hug when you are struggling.

During a conversation about discrimination,
someone mentions that they are Jewish and
the Good Man, now drunk, says,
"Maybe if you were a foreigner it would count,
maybe if you wore one of the funny little hats it would
count. But you're nothing."
My throat goes dread-dry, shocked hoarse.

He knows that I am also Jewish. Still, he says this
looking right at me with a broadening smile,
like he is letting me in on the sweetest joke.

Later, when I give the toast
l'chaim tovim ul'shalom,

he asks me, "What is that gibberish?
Use real words." When he leaves, he hugs me,

says, "Goodnight, brother."
It's funny, this new definition of *brother*.
It stings—tastes like ash.

Some weeks later, the first time I tell this story on
stage, the Good Man is there. He is the first to come up to me after and
says, "I can't believe someone said that, what an asshole."

For a moment, just long enough to decide this is
more important than our friendship, I am silent.
Then I tell him, "It was you, you said that."

He apologizes. We talk it out. By the end,
we laugh. When he leaves he calls me brother again.
It still tastes of ash

We still get excited when we see each other.
But I don't invite him to parties anymore,
and he doesn't call me brother.

He was drunk for both conversations.
It's been years. I wonder if he even remembers.
I still know he is a Good Man. It still stings.

ASL

I have spent the last 32 years learning
to manipulate my native language.

I used to think this is what
made me special; now I worry

that I have learned to manipulate words so well
that even I can't tell when I am lying.

I am learning American Sign Language.
I only started doing it to flirt with a girl.

There are certainly better reasons to learn
something, but I can't think of any more honest.

In ASL, to miss an object, you move one hand,
grasping like it just slipped by you.

But to miss a person, you point two fingers, barrel-sure,
at your own chin, like, without them, living is pointless.

I don't know if there is a sign for missing
yourself, for missing who you used to be.

But if I don't learn to use my words more openly,
more honestly, I am going to need one.

WARNING TO TRAVELERS

Candlelight is the fastest way to travel. —Neil Gaiman

We focus too much on the purpose of things
and watch them too little. We all know that
a candle can produce light and heat, that, if
careless, it can devour your whole world.

As adults we seem to forget that even
the inanimate can be alive, that breath
is not the only kind of living.
We ignore the shadows, the constant flicker.

I am engineer enough to know
that if there was magic in this world,
we have long since scienced it into
extinction. We cannot actually fall into
the light and suddenly be somewhere else.

But that constant flicker,
that rapid accident of shadow
and air current, if watched
with the patience of a believer
and the fervor a child,
can produce anything.

Be careful watching the fire—
it is far more dangerous than
touching it. Our minds will take us where
we need to go, careless of the burn.

TO THE YOUNG MAN WHO ONLY TALKS ABOUT HIMSELF IN IMAGE AND METAPHOR,

who believes
that once a metaphor is
explained, it becomes pointless.

We are a lot alike.
And you are dead wrong.

I too know what it means
to have the jaws of a wolf
and the cheeks of a pufferfish.
To have a nasty bite
and still be full of hot air.

I know that chainsaws can laugh,
that everything that cuts loves to laugh.
This is why we learned to talk so pretty,
why we learned never to chuckle,
always to guffaw. To turn our mouths
into church bells.

The problem is that steel wrapped in velvet
is still steel. It will never keep anyone comfortable.

I know that having a big heart doesn't mean
you have a full one. It is amazing how lonely
can become a symphony when no one is there
to hear it.

We both have a lot of good reasons to be angry.
We know that snowflakes and death
are perfect analogues. Both are always unique
and so cold.

If dead loved ones walk behind us,
then heaven is empty.
And we are choirmasters.

But the reason that you are stuck
and I am building the life I always dreamed,
the difference between an angry boy
and a proud man, is that eventually
the metaphors have to stop.

I have a mouth made of trumpets
and a belly full of people who said I couldn't,
but my spine is just my spine.

You wondered what it would be like
if the legends were real.
I am the phoenix.
Alone to this.
Broken to this.

We think of flame
as dangerous. But without the light,
we cannot see. It is fire that keeps us alive
through the night and fed through the cold.

We have both been ash;
now we get to be the light.
Stop wallowing in the dirt, my friend,
and welcome this well-earned burn.

THINGS I HAVE BEEN TOLD AFTER PERFORMING: A FOUND POEM

You are nothing like I thought you'd be.
Your poems are so big,
I thought you would be taller.

I don't like how angry you are. You would
be more attractive if you didn't yell so much.
Come home with me.

The way you talk about death
makes me love you.

I think it's irresponsible,
the way you tell people to be okay with
being fat and angry.

Are you really Jewish? I mean really, like
actually Jewish?
Prove it. Say some Hebrew for me.
See, I knew you weren't REALLY Jewish.

Hold me.
Take me now.

I don't trust anyone who talks for a living.

I loved your work,
but you are so smart,
why do you write poems?
You could be doing something important.

ROPE

A tiny bit of honesty is
a dangerous thing.
But the truth, wound around
itself over and over,
is a solid, lasting, worthy feat,
a life worth living for.

BEING JEWISH MEANS ALWAYS BEING TOO MUCH OR NOT ENOUGH 2

I meet a woman in a bar who is so proud of being
an activist that it almost hurts to look at her—
she believes her own good nature
sunshine enough to solve world hunger.
She never says the word *gentle*
but it oozes out of her. I can hear it
between every word: "I wish that this world *gentle*
was *gentle* a *gentle* safer *gentle* place *gentle* for *gentle*
everyone." When I mention that I am Jewish,
all of the kindness drains out of her face,
her rosy cheeks and welcoming grin
replaced with a shark's smile
as she asks, "Are you a Zionist?"

I say no, but she isn't satisfied. "Seriously, what do
you think of Israel?" I sigh, knowing that the comradery
of the evening is about to end. I say, it's complicated.
I think that everyone deserves a home. A place where
they can not only be safe, but feel safe. Everyone.

"Disgusting," she says. "Ridiculous," she says,
smiling sweetly at the taste of her own hate.

I deeply wish she was the first sensitive, welcoming,
tender-heart to tell me I should be ashamed of being
Jewish, but anti-Semitism lives as deeply in the
smile as it does the fist.

TOXICITY

Super glue was originally intended
as an emergency field suture to prevent
soldiers from bleeding to death.
The project was a partial success—

it kept them from bleeding to death
but poisoned their blood, killed them anyway.

Relationships can be just like that.
When one is sick, trying to save it
can poison your everything.

To be happy, we must all
learn to be surgeons, to cut
away that which cannot be cured.

APRIL 16, 2007

when i visit the wikipedia page about your murder,
it takes me almost five minutes to find your name.
it is tucked deep among the list of the 31 other victims.

i hate that word. victim. it's so small. words
should have to be as big as the concept they describe.
whatever word we replace victim with should take as long to say as it
took me to find your name.

there you are. Henry Lee, number 16.
it took me so long to find you because they used your

government name, your american name,
the one your parents thought would keep you
safe. even though i never heard anyone
call you anything other than Henh.

Henh Lee
Henh
Henh

when i type your name, Henh Lee, into google,
i find a thousand living people with your name
and no mention of you. i spend hours looking at their photos to see if
any of them have your smile
so i can hate them. call them thief.

when i type Henry Lee into google,
i find the wikipedia page about your murderer.

the thing i hate most about being human
isn't our penchant for violence; it's
the fact that we won't be remembered
for the lives we lead, only for the
person who made us this way.

despite all the death i have seen—
how often i have wanted to bring someone back—
i have always hated all frankenstein stories.
no one seems to care or even remember

frankenstein was the scientist.
the creation was nameless,
nameless like you feel now, Henh.
the wikipedia page about the virginia tech massacre
is 12,000 words long. less than 500 are dedicated to
the 32 who were murdered. the rest are about him.
about the man who made you nameless.

JEWDAISM

שְׁמַע יִשְׂרָאֵל יְהוָה אֱלֹהֵינוּ יְהוָה אֶחָד*

We Jews are called the people of the book.
I can read Hebrew, but I do not
understand it.

I was taught that in order to become an adult,
that in order to become a man, I needed to develop
a connection with the language of my ancestors.
That I needed to be able to read the holy Torah.

I have spent my whole life trying to be
a good human,
a good man,
and a good Jew
in that order.

This has left me so much to learn
that I haven't gotten to Hebrew yet.

If I know anything about my ancestors, it's
that they would have a definite opinion about this
and that they would not keep their mouths shut.
They couldn't—they would tell me
exactly what they thought of my choices.

I wouldn't understand a damn word.
I was taught that following tradition
is more important than understanding it.

When it comes to Judaism,
I am a jukebox.
I can't interpret,

---

* She-ma yisrael, adonai eloheinu, adonai echad
  Hear O' Israel, the Lord is our Gd, the Lord is One.

but I will play the sounds
of my ancestors
over
and over
     and over
^{**}אַשְׁרֵי יוֹשְׁבֵי בֵיתֶךָ, עוֹד יְהַלְלוּךָ סֶּלָה

** Ash-rei yosh-vei vei-te-cha - od y'-ha-l'-lu-cha se-la
   Happy are those who dwell in Your house; they are continually praising You.

TINY WORDS

Some words have meaning
entirely out of proportion with their size.
     Want
         Need
   Alone
These words get easier to say the farther you are from
home.

There is an instinctual
need to escape moments
of high adrenaline.
There is a reason that
the big moments we control never happen at home:
the proposals, the breakups.

   Love
     Die
This is why death is so traumatic—
we tend to discover it at home,
where we have nowhere to run but the unknown.

When something terrible happens
outside, you can run home.

   Help   Please

Be careful of the words you say there.
They are naked and forever.

Hope
           Dream
    Heal

WHIMSY

When an Engineer needs to make a wish,
they find an excuse. Calls it a blue moon—
says it only happens once every four years,
that this tradition goes back at least 700 years.

They love logic the way others love their children;
it is their everything. But on the days
when it isn't enough, whimsy is their last refuge.

When the Artist tells them she doesn't understand
why they are all excited about a blue moon,
that, after all, it's nothing special, I mean full moons
happen all the time, right? It's not even blue.
The Engineer doesn't know how to tell her
that it is the wish that matters, not the excuse.

They never understood birthday parties.
The whole keeping a wish a secret so it comes
true thing always seemed ridiculous.
If you are relying on superstition and hope
to make your dreams come true,
then doesn't it make sense to have
everyone possible hoping?

Even when they invest in whimsy,
the Engineer relies on logic.
They don't tell the Artist their wish;

she laughs at their whimsy enough.
When belief is already an ill-fitting shirt,
being laughed at is too much.

THINGS I CAN'T BELIEVE WE DON'T HAVE WORDS FOR

If the act of naming something is
an attempt to give it purpose, then
leaving it nameless is more than a mere
act of laziness—it is
an attempt to rob
it of all meaning.

Killing your own twin.

The desire to watch everything burn,
even though you hate the flame,
the light, the smell.

An appropriate amount of pride in one's
own actions.

The taste in your mouth,
one sugar cube sweeter than blood,
when you know someone can't be trusted
but have no idea why.

The urge to jump every time you are
at a fatal ledge, even though you have never
wanted more to live.

For a gathering of mourners.

For the reason you don't give up,
no matter how bloody and tired.

For how good a failure can feel
when you never thought you could
get this far.

For the feeling somewhere between
fear and ecstasy right before you confess
how you feel.

Homesickness not for a place but for a time.

The desire to kiss someone you have no interest in,
just to see how they taste, how their tongue moves.

The first time you hold a new niece or nephew.

We have more than a thousand words for the things
that scare us, whole dictionaries
worth of phobias, but the sensations
we worry we could get lost in
remain nameless and lurking.

A LETTER TO ARIZONA FROM
THE AMERICAN FLAG

In April 2010, Arizona wrote into law an act which not only enabled but required police officers to stop anyone they have "reason" to suspect of being an illegal immigrant, thus signing into law racial profiling for the first time since separate but equal was declared inherently unequal. The law was declared unconstitutional by the Supreme Court, but the legacy of hate and distrust remain.

Please, I beg of you,
take me down
and burn me.
This is the last patriotic act I will
ever ask of you. I do not want to
fly over your post offices
and schoolyards anymore.
Don't you wish *patriot* sounded a little less like
Klansman when coming out of your mouth?

Please, take me down and
cut one star out of my center.
You are not worthy of being a part of me anymore,
Arizona.

I have been used to hide terrible deeds:
I have flown over Baghdad,
over Abu Ghraib, over Guantanamo Bay.
I am done being the excuse for blood and torture.
I am done having my stripes be the prison bars
separating man from the sky.
We are supposed to be a country of dreamers,
America, where a person can make
something out of nothing.
When did you forget that?
I have petitioned the sky;
I have requested that next 4th of July

the wind be as calm as your conscience.
I will not fly over your parades.
Your celebration deserves to be a moment of silence
for the hypocrisy you have shown here.

It is tradition for all fallen soldiers to be buried
with an American flag as a symbol that their country
will never forget them.

As long as I am being used to justify this
mockery of patriotism, I am not worthy of this honor.
I ask instead that all the fallen be buried with a letter
apologizing that this country
can no longer live up to their sacrifice.

I will never rise for your hatred,
your racism, again.

BEING JEWISH MEANS ALWAYS BEING TOO MUCH OR NOT ENOUGH 3

At a comedy show, someone mentions
Moses, and the rest of the night becomes a flurry of
Jew jokes. It quickly becomes clear that the only
things the performers know about being Jewish
is that our language sounds likes spitting
and that their religion uses all of our
stories. We are nothing but a first draft.
Something that had a purpose once but is
just taking up space now.

I can hear it in the way
they say the word *Jew*—
they say it just like
I say AOL: with
emphasis and a rising lilt.

Surely that's a joke, right?
No one cares about that anymore.

I STILL MISS YOU

When a fire is trapped,
slowly eating itself to nothing,
still hate-hot but running out of
oxygen, it will start to breathe.
The smoke that has been slowly leaking
out of the tiniest cracks will start to
pull back inside. This monster,
so hungry for air it pulses,
makes even the most experienced
firefighters nervous.

This inhale is the only warning of a backdraft.
If it happens, it is not the flame you need
initially fear. It is the act of combustion.

Creating that much fire can literally suck
the air from your lungs.
When you reflexively breathe back in,
the superheated air sears the lungs,
destroying your body's ability to absorb oxygen.

This will be the last breath you ever take.

Goodbyes
are exactly like that—
no matter how ready you think
you are for them,
they always leave you with so
many things you want to say.

You will never get a chance.

SIREN

When I read the legends, I marvel
at how many different types of sirens
there must have been.
Not all men ache
for the same song.

Every human has a torch they are willing
to moth themselves into. Every city has a
voice, a specific type of person it calls.

Prague speaks to the builders,
to people who know that to create
something new on rubble is not to replace
the history, but to add—
a brick-and-bone harmony.

New York is for people who have something
to prove, each of us howling at our own moon.

Whenever I visit a place that makes words
like comfortable and settle spill accident
from my mouth, all of my joints scream.
Say, *Don't even think about it,*
you are a creature of yearn.
Stretch, boy, stretch.

HERO

The difference between a good man
and a great one is the ability to be crying
and still proud,

to be out of breath, unable to
make a sound and still know
you are all song.

THINGS TO DO WHEN NOT TAKING
YOUR SLEEPING PILLS

Tell yourself that you do not need them,
that you are better off without them.

Second-guess your every decision.
Start with the small ones—which shampoo
you use, what percentage milk you put in your
cereal. This will make it easier to properly judge
yourself for the big ones when you get there.

Write the seventh version of a poem
you know you will never share; there are
some things you are not willing to admit yet.

Tell yourself that you do not need your sleeping
pills, that you are better off without them.

Masturbate—do not allow this to become
about pleasure or release.
Make this only about motion,
about your mind conquering your body at least once.

Do not look at the lower right-hand drawer of your
desk. If you even glance at it, you will spend
hours going through old photos, separating them
into the piles of memories you love and those
you'd rather forget. Those piles are never
the same, so you remember everything.

Admit why you do not take your sleeping pills:
the only time your brain gets quiet is when it is
sleep addled.

Forgive yourself these tiny acts of self-destruction.
Watch the sunrise for the fourth time this week.
Allow the new day to give you hope.

Tell yourself that you do not need your sleeping pills, that you are better off without them. Try to believe it this time.

The Engineer
Makes a Flowchart

I need music the way
most people need water,

> which is
> to say

frequently and pure.

I need water the way
most people need love,

> which is
> to say

the dirty kind is just fine.

I am not looking for it
but I see it everywhere.
Its taste is always on
my tongue.

> which is
> to say

I need love the way
a man on a hunger strike
needs food,

I need my tongue the way
a liar needs the truth.

> which is
> to say

desperately,
you cannot be
that far from something
unless you cling to it.

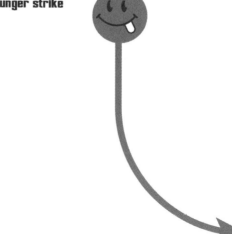

mostly at night,
when the fear
of not knowing
is worse than
the fear of believing.

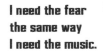

I need the fear
the same way
I need the music.

which is
to say

I need the truth the way
a true believer needs Gd,

They are the only things
that keep me from
walking into the sunrise
and burning,
      just burning.

SILENCE

Samantha,
I wouldn't change a thing about our prom night,
not even my ridiculous ███████████ tuxedo.
I have spent so many ████████ wishing we could have had a different
ending. I have lost track of the number
of times I called you crazy, and every time I did, I was
so ███████████ of myself.

Do you remember that night when we watched
the meteor shower and you put my hand on your
left breast and offered me ████? I still can't ████ ████
all I could say was ████.

Dad.
You are the ██ of ██ I have ever met.
Thank you. I wouldn't be half the ██ I am today
if it wasn't for you. Remember
what you said to me when I came
home with a broken arm? You said, "Jared, why
don't you just ███████." And I did Dad, I have spent
the rest of my life trying to ████████████
so that you would be ████ of me.

If I ever have kids I am going to make sure
they know one thing. I am going to make sure they know
███
and it's all because of you, Dad.

The first time a woman told me I was the only
fat man she had ever wanted to fuck, I could only say
████████████████████. I almost married her.
By the third time a woman told me I was the only fat
man she had ever wanted to fuck, I knew to say
████████████████████.
I think a lot about the other women I've loved,

the ones who never told me why I was desirable
and I ██ that if they did, they'd say ████████ .

The thing about the truth is that it is
almost never one thing.
I just want to be an honest man
while still leaving room for **all** the answers.
So how come every time I try to hold the truth, it
████████████████ .

BROKENHEARTED BUT STILL FULL OF HOPE, THE ENGINEER TRIES TO BUILD A PERFECT HEART

He wishes he could use his own,
but nothing this easy to break,
nothing this tiny and close to meat
could possibly be where love
springs from.

The engineer builds a proper vessel.
Large and delicate. Made of steel
but still fragile. He knows it will need
an engine.

He rules out combustion—as much
as love feels the unannounced detonation
of fireworks, we cannot build
a solid foundation using this much fury
and destruction.

The engineer rules out solar power.
The world is a dark place, and it wouldn't
do for the heart to stop functioning
when it is needed most.

Willing to sacrifice efficiency
for elegance, he settles on an older method:
steam power and clockwork. What
could be more like love than the graceful
turning of one thing into another?
What a perfect transformation of energy!
What could be more intimate than the handhold
of gear turning gear, the rhythmic thump
of turning hope into love?

ADVICE FROM MY INNER PUNK ROCK
WE SHOULD ALL TAKE

Never dye your hair a color
quieter than your heart.
If you have to be soft, do it honestly.

When they tell you
you are too loud,
smile, dig deep, and
show them the true meaning of volume.

We were given two lungs and only one heart.
This is a rare opportunity to let the truth
do the work of the metaphor.

Punk rock has never been
about what you were screaming
and always about how loud you could be.
Prove to yourself you have a voice,

then find a good use for it.
Understand the similarities
between the power chord

and the heartbeat, between
the silence and the noise.
We are all both the fury and the stillness.
To break is human.

To roar is human.
But to never stop
is the holy in all of us.

BEER

The first girl I ever fell in love with
was named Samantha. I didn't drink
my first beer until four years after
I had kissed her goodbye.

But still every time I drink a good IPA,
I think of her. The first sip of an India pale ale
is always a gut-kick of bitter so intense
you wonder why the fuck you
ordered it in the first place,
but as soon as you are about to spit it out,
it turns to a mellow sweetness,
all the more enjoyable because of your
previous discomfort.

My grandfather hated beer—
he liked his liquor as straight as his spine.
But still whenever I drink to his memory,
it is always a porter.
A porter can be intimidating,
just like my grandfather,
it can't be seen through;
you never knew how he felt till he told you.
But the thing that lasts the longest about a porter,
about my grandfather, is the aroma.
It has been 10 years since we put him in the ground,
but still every time I hug anyone, I swear
they must be wearing his cologne.

When I tell my friends
that everything in my life can
relate back to beer, they chuckle,
say, "You might have a problem."

I'm not saying I drink a beer
for every situation—I am saying
I understand the small magic
of heat and change.

In all of human language,
there are only seven thousand
words for love, but more than
12 million types of beer.

If you take hops, sugar, and water,
add heat, take strangers and time,
add *we will get through this*,
the end result is so much more
than its parts.

If you think you can find the exact right words
to make someone feel about themselves the
way you do, then by all means, speak the words.
I would rather pass them a beer.

When the time finally comes to say
goodbye to me for the last time,
don't hurt yourself trying to
sum up everything you want to say.

Raise a glass, drink it down.
I'll be listening.

GROWING OLD
For my wife

You love me just as I am. I never had a reason
to lose weight until you. I can't stand the
idea that my body is the only thing
that could come between us.
I want to be just a little
less me so we can
have a little
more time.

THE LAST LOVE LETTER FROM AN ENTOMOLOGIST

Dear Samantha,
I'm sorry, but we have to get a divorce.
I know that seems like an odd way
to start a love letter,
but let me explain.
It's not you,
it's definitely not me,
it's just human beings don't love
as well as insects do.

I love you far too much to let what we have
be ruined by the failings of our species.
So instead
I'm going to leave you now
while I still remember you fondly.

I saw the way you looked at the waiter last night.
I know you would never do anything,
you never do, but still,
I saw the way you looked
at the waiter last night.

Did you know that when a female fly
accepts the pheromones put off by a male
it rewrites her brain, destroys the
receptors for pheromones?
Sensing the change,
the male fly does the same.

When flies love each other,
they do it so hard
that they can never love
anything else ever again.
If either one dies before procreation,

that is the end of both sets of genetic code.
Now *that* is dedication.

After breaking up with Elizabeth,
we spent three days dividing
everything we had bought together,
like if I knew which pots were mine,
like if I knew which drapes were mine,
the pain would go away.

When two praying mantises mate,
the nervous system of the male
begins to shut down.
While he still has control over his motor functions,
he flips onto his back,
exposing his soft underbelly
to his lover like a gift.
She then proceeds to lovingly,
and I *do* mean lovingly,
dice him into tiny pieces,
shoveling each piece into her mouth,
wasting not a single morsel—
even the exoskeleton must go.
She does this so that
when their children are born
she has a first meal to regurgitate to feed them.
Now that is dedication.

I could never do that for you.
So I have a new plan.
I will spend the rest of my life
committing petty injustices.
I will jaywalk at every opportunity.
I will steal things I could easily afford.
I will be rude to strangers.

I hope you will do the same.
I hope reincarnation is real.

I hope that these petty crimes
cause me to be reborn as a lesser creature.
I hope we are reborn as flies
so that we can love each other
as hard as we were meant to.

PERSONAL SOUNDTRACK

I like to imagine there is a quiet guitar
playing behind everything I do.

Okay, sometimes that guitar
is a cello, and sometimes quiet
is excruciatingly loud,
but I like to imagine there is a
single instrument playing
behind everything I do.

When your hands are old tools,
rusted and worn from heavy use,
when your lips are a dirty secret,
when your confidence changes
as rapidly as the weather,

you learn to hold on to the days
when you can fully believe in yourself
like they are holy.
Like they make faith unnecessary.
Like they are proof of Gd.

I had seven of them last January,
four in February,
only one in March,
but April was a good month—
I had sixty-four of those
days in total last year.
You gave me seven of them
in a row.

When I am with you,
I like to imagine that
there are two instruments
playing behind everything we do:

one of them is quiet,
the other excruciatingly loud.
I can hear them both,
they play the same tune,
this is my favorite kind of music.

ARTIFACTS
After Warehouse 13

Sometimes when a person loves an object,
it becomes a part of them. Sometimes when
a person hates a thing, it becomes family.

Sometimes when a person is too much person
for one body, it leaks into the inanimate, creating magic.

I wouldn't suggest you test this, but I promise
if you sit near anything radioactive, you will
hear Oppenheimer's voice saying sorry over and over.

His regret is so strong it will break your body down.
Listen close enough to a Geiger counter,

its clicks become Einstein saying, "I told you so,
I told you so." Why do you think rich men buy the
instruments of famous musicians

and put them behind glass instead of playing them?
To protect a valuable object? Do you see their
families in cases? Their egos? Their legacies?

When they touch the instrument, they feel the music.
A language they never taught their hearts to hear.

Imagine a subway, rush-hour sardined, and everyone
on it is screaming in a language you don't know
but yearn to. It is enough to drive you mad.

They buy the instrument, hoping it will give
them the life they wish they had chosen,

only to find they cannot hold it. Of course it goes behind
glass. This is why so many of us keep the things
given to us by the dead but so rarely touch them.

We need to believe there is a piece of them still
inside the object, are afraid to prove ourselves right.

I FALL IN LOVE LIKE PUNK ROCK

Fast and awkward
like nobody taught me
how to use this instrument
I call a body,
but I knew it was important,
so I did it anyway.

I need you like power chords—
you are loud in all of the right ways,
you keep the static quiet,
you help cover up my mistakes.

I have always been your drum kit.
Even with your whole body,
I don't understand
how you make me beat so fast.

You are the cheap whiskey
in all of my songs.
No matter what I am
talking about,
I always come back to you.
Be it politics, or a party,
or what I want to be
when I grow up.

It's 1986 and we are The Clash
on the day they realized they didn't have
to stare at their feet anymore.
That a love like ours is a music
worth listening to, or

it's 1977 and we are the Sex Pistols
two weeks after first being banned
from the charts, the first time

they were caught smiling in a group photo,
as if to say—

it doesn't matter
if you censor us—
we have already changed
everything.
We will make this awkward legendary.

Maybe, if we are lucky,
it's forever,
and we are the Misfits.
We have taken our very name from
Marilyn Monroe's last movie.
Our very existence
has taken their pop icon,
their beauty, their flavor of the month
and made it fast and dirty and so much more.

There is no need for this rabid-dog lonely.
The critics, once they were done calling
us irrelevant noise,
called us beautiful and desperate.

We are desperate and beautiful.
We are living proof that if you do something hard enough, fast enough,
for long enough,
they will not only forgive you
your shortcomings,
they will love you for them.

LOVE 1A:

Love can only be described
the way it is lived. In parts.

Hoping that the whole makes sense,
even though we know none of the pieces do.

Love 1A:
Love *is* a sandwich. Everything we do can be
reduced to the layering on of parts, hoping
we get the combination right.

Love *is* a sandwich. Both are silly little things
that we created. We put both in our mouths.

Love 1B:
I love like a tornado;
here we will be safe.
But around us,
things will be destroyed
by our excess, and I promise, we will not end
up in the same place that we started.

Love 1C:
If there is anything more like the way I fall in love
than a children's cartoon, I haven't found it yet.

There are eight women who say
that I am the perfect man,
that any woman would be lucky to have me.
I have asked three of them out.
They all said no. We still hang out,

but boy it gets awkward sometimes.
If there's anything more like a painting

of a tunnel on a wall than this,
I haven't found it yet.

Love 2:
Love is the only thing that
ALL of the songs are right about.
Love *is* all you need.
Love *is* a cold and broken hallelujah.

Love 3:
The heart is a terrible metaphor
for love; please
stop using it. Love is not a muscle.
It cannot atrophy from lack of use.
Love is an organ—it can always sneak up on you.

The lungs are a much better metaphor for love.

The inhale is that moment
of excitement when you meet someone special.
The exhale, that feeling of hate we all fear we will feel
if it doesn't work out.

But the holding, that moment
when your body is all potential. That is love.

BEEKEEPER

I knew I loved you the day you mentioned
the beekeepers.

You said a bee's sting is a sensitizer,
that every time you are stung it hurts
just a little less. There are beekeepers
out there whose bodies are so full of poison,
they can't even feel it.

I don't know if your story
was true—you are the only person whose facts
I never bothered to check.

You said bee venom was a sensitizer,
which makes it possible for your own
body's defenses to turn against it.
That one sting too many
could kill that beekeeper before he even felt
the prick.

You said love is exactly like that,
a tiny poison that filled you up by parts
until it was so much a part of who you were
that to remove or add even the tiniest bit
must surely be fatal.

That's why you wanted it so badly.
You were the only disaster
I never wanted to say no to,
chocolate-covered arsenic.
I knew I was over you
when you said, *You know
you could never be happy
with any girl who wasn't at least
a little bit wrong for you.*

I said you're right,
but I hear they are coating
other poisons in sugar these days.
That it is even possible to become immune
to cyanide. I want to know what it's like
to taste almonds without having to crush
something between my teeth.

LIVING TRUST,
OR THE PROPER USE OF MY BODY

To my nephew Harrison, I leave
my throat. It is the only part
of myself I have ever considered
perfect. It knows when to swallow
and when to speak. It will help
you be the right amount of assertive.

To the last woman I loved, I leave my bones.
They are broken but still work.
Just like you, like your conscience.
Please take them apart, learn how to be
whole, use any of the pieces you need.
I have long since forgiven your lies.
I have long since forgiven my body
for failing, for breaking. Maybe forgiveness
is transitive.

To my niece Tallulah, I leave my ears.
Sound is the only thing in this universe
that lasts forever, my dear. You will
know how to put these to good use.
I know you will always be careful
with what you say, what you allow them
to hear.

To my fiancée, I leave my skin.
It is stretched and tattooed. Many
people have looked at my skin
and thought it ruined. Just like
you have looked at yourself and
thought the worst, but you are soft
and gentle and contain everything you need,
just like this skin did for me.

To my friends, I leave my teeth.
They are broken and ugly and for
that I apologize, but they are the parts
of myself I worried about the most.
Just like I worried about you all.
Bear these as a reminder to take
care of each other.

To my own memory, I leave my words.
They are far from perfect and were frequently
misused, but they were heartfelt and honest.
The only legacy I could ever accept.

ACKNOWLEDGEMENTS

Thank you so much to those who helped this book come to be. Thank you, Tiffany Woodley, for your edits and support. Thank you to Johnathan Weiskopf for recommending a brilliant photographer for the cover. Thank you, David Benthal, for doing an amazing cover photo. Thank you to my entire family, and most specifically to Amanda Singer for your support through the process of getting this book published. Thank you to Brendan Constantine, Mike McMgee, and Chris August for your support. Thank you, Rico Frederick, for your edits and your design of the flowchart.

Thank you to Wes Mongo Jolley, who put my work on the IndieFeed Podcast repeatedly, and Jeffrey Kay, who consistently videotaped and published my work. If it wasn't for your support and the way you both helped me get my name out, I would never have even tried to publish a book.

Thank you to the entire Button organization, and most specifically to Hitomi Wong, without whom this book would never have been completed.

Thank you to the following journals for first publishing poems that appear in this book: *Danse Macabre* for "A letter to Sarah," *Great Weather for Media* for "Love 1A)," *Union Station Magazine* for "Exchange Rates," *IndieFeed Podcast* for "An Entomologist's Last Love Letter."

JARED SINGER is an audio engineer and poet currently living in New Jersey. He grew up in the Blue Ridge Mountains of Virginia, and came to maturity in Brooklyn. This life has taught Jared that both beauty and hardship will find us wherever we go, and we cannot hide from either. What we can do is choose which we look for and which we focus our life around. Jared is proud to have his poems focus on joy, science, and learning from his worst moments.

OTHER BOOKS BY BUTTON POETRY

If you enjoyed this book, please consider checking out some of our others, below. Readers like you allow us to keep broadcasting and publishing. Thank you!

Neil Hilborn, *Our Numbered Days*
Hanif Abdurraqib, *The Crown Ain't Worth Much*
Olivia Gatwood, *New American Best Friend*
Donte Collins, *Autopsy*
Melissa Lozada-Oliva, *peluda*
Sabrina Benaim, *Depression & Other Magic Tricks*
William Evans, *Still Can't Do My Daughter's Hair*
Rudy Francisco, *Helium*
Guante, *A Love Song, A Death Rattle, A Battle Cry*
Rachel Wiley, *Nothing Is Okay*
Neil Hilborn, *The Future*
Phil Kaye, *Date & Time*
Andrea Gibson, *Lord of the Butterflies*
Blythe Baird, *If My Body Could Speak*
Desireé Dallagiacomo, *SINK*
Dave Harris, *Patricide*
Michael Lee, *The Only Worlds We Know*
Raych Jackson, *Even the Saints Audition*
Brenna Twohy, *Swallowtail*
Porsha Olayiwola, *i shimmer sometimes, too*

Available at buttonpoetry.com/shop and more!